La

DEDICATED TO THE MOST BEAUTIFUL SINGLE LOVERS WHO CARE ABOUT YOU WITHOUT WORDS TO TELL, SMILE TO EXPRESS, AND FEAR ON YOUR THOUGHT

#Where's my love

Last Without Anything

#Where's my love

Last Without Anything

A Untold Love Story written by
Arya Ramachandran

Feel the love

#Where's my love

Last Without Anything

#Where's my love

Last Without Anything

Copyright©
Written by or Author **Arya Ramachandran**
Last Without Anything
First edition Book

#Where's my love

Last Without Anything

#Where's my love

Last Without Anything

ACKNOWLEDGEMENT

This is a fiction novel. Were by non of the roles or any living form that is being described in this book represent or depicts any other living form either living or dead.

All the roles and their behavior along with their respective dialogues are pure fiction.

Non of the words in the dialogues represent to humiliate any form of life.

This short story is a romantic emotional thought of the main character. It has various character throughout the book.

This short story has humor, comedy, romance, affections, feeling, young adult life contents.

Non of the characters in the play represent any form This story is made for entertainment purpose only. Enjoy reading!

#Where's my love

Last Without Anything

#Where's my love

ABOUT THE AUTHOR

Arya Ramachandran is a teenager who spent his entire childhood developing creative stories and writing them into poems, song lyrics, short stories, and even novels.

He owns his own book series by the name, "An ARC Series."

Do follow him in Instagram - @arya_the_author for more updates on upcoming short stories, poem and novels release.

Do share your experice with the book to your family, friends and romance reader friends. They would love to read an epic.

#Where's my love

Last Without Anything

#Where's my love

#Where's my love

It was during tuition when I got a notification ting on my phone. It was Arjun, a good informer about all the school activities to me. He had a very important message coated in bold.

I skipped the distracted teacher and hid the phone behind my bag, to check the message, to read what the bold message was.

Within the sleepiness in my mind, for a holiday morning class. I read the message, so deep and clear as it made more hurts for each letter I read in my mind.

For a longest of the school days, I had a special something something for a girl.

She ain't that pretty. She was colored and not a charter buster for any soul around in school. I got a lot of questions as to why her but I smiled with the answer that I couldn't explain.

#Where's my love

Last Without Anything

The date, venue, time, location - I don't know. But I just like her a lot, I just really like her a lot. I look at her about a dozen times a day without even realizing that it's happening; subconsciously. But she was beautiful to me.

She had a name, not that long and not that short either. She didn't know that I had something for her, that all boys don't look for in a girl when they date. That something was special indeed.

She was helpful, kind, soft hearted, and she was like everything to me. The most beautiful and loving person in the world.

The message I got destroyed years of deep care and thoughts.

"Aarti left our school." said Arjun's message in bold. Led to a bold shock to me.

I gulped my saliva and tried to control my eyes before I could breakdown in tuition.

I looked to my left and right in plight. I showed the message to both Sajay and Varun.

#Where's my love

Last Without Anything

They looked at each other surprised. Kept a hand on my shoulder saying, "Leave her Shyam… You are better with some other who likes you back than her."

I returned his hand back to Sajay's shoulder saying, "I want to meet her now."

Sajay looked around the room, "I got an idea… you be calm…" he said turning to Varun, "Will you do me a favour right now?"

Varun nodded.

Sajay whispered something and they both got into their phones and I thanked Arjun for informing me about the resignation of the beauty from our unholy structure.

"Her house location… I got it." Varun said, showing me his phone with the map ready.

"I'll get a call." Sajay said. "For a minute study… we will leave soon."

He opened his book again and handed his smile to me. I didn't understand whose call, but I got back into studying, as he said for a minute.

#Where's my love

Just before the second clock passed 30 on the plane wall, a call dropped by Sajay's phone. It rung straight and loud to everyone's ears. That was the call.

He pulled his phone out and answered, "Hello Amma..." he said and hummed in short lines for couple of second, "Ohh! Okay! Then I will come."

The teacher questioned him, "What's the matter Sajay? Why did your mother call you?"

"Mom... She said that we had an appointment with the doc Mathew for my dental... We have to leave... I'll drop Varun and Shyam at theirs on the way and visit the doc." He explained to the teacher and also to me.

Everything, all of a sudden came into total connections.

I found that greatest idea which Sajay took to help me out.

It all made a ton of sense to me; all of a second second.

#Where's my love

Last Without Anything

We packed our bags, stuffing all the books in uneven order and walked out of the teacher's room, as soon as possible.

Varun turned on the maps and it took to us running on the side of the road.

We three ran with our bags hanging and jumping on our backs. We ran straight towards what we thought was her house, more than a mile apart from tuition.

We actually ran by the side of the road, as fast as we could. I had so much expectations, filled up in my mind on the way of run.

I stopped all of a sudden imitating a long breath. I felt suffocating to catch a good breath. I stopped. I bend down resting my red palm on my knee joint, inhaling and exhaling like a bad dragon breathing.

Varun and Sajay running in front of me, stopped when they heard two foot sounds less on the sand and stone platform. They turned back at me.

#Where's my love

Sajay said pulling me, motivating me back to run, "Yo... No time for breathing... You got a girl to catch... Run!" He shouted.

I left the breathlessness and the thought that gave the same. I ran.

I was pretty sure some of the drivers in the car would think us to be bare bunkers for running with bags and together with too much excitement.

We reached, what the map said was her building. I was felt with overwhelming desire and love for her.

I used to beat up the person who talked bad about her. I used to look at her for no reason and give her a sudden smile.

I stood in front looking at her house, for it was the building, I lived three years back. Filled up with nostalgic feeling.

We ran towards the left of the building, in and pressed the button and waited for the lift of teleports to arrive at our start.

#Where's my love

Last Without Anything

We entered in and I found myself breathing heavily. My heart sunk into unidentified fear. I had to tell her that I love her. I had to tell her what I had in my mind for her. I wanted her to know everything.

I got so excited.

Someone will leave your life, just like that. But they will not know what they were to you. I found the need for her to know about me.

The fourth floor rung a triple ting sound as the door of the lift opened up.

We turned right and stood in front of flat 43. I felt terrible and nostalgic. I lived her for 15 years in this very street, this very building, this very flat with the number 43.

I grew up from a child, lost it in the same place. The bedroom was limited to one but the world this flat gave me, is still wonders.

Varun pointed me towards the bell.

I pressed on it with a lot of effort. The bell torque was hard. One needed to apply more

#Where's my love

pressure to ring it right and perfectly. It was the same as before.

I remember myself trying to press the bell button as a child but I couldn't, as a child. My father would smile at me, looking so tall, as he pressed the bell and my mom opened the door with a smile to hug me, back from my intense nursery class.

I rung the bell hard.

My mind had a thousand words to say. My heart was beating terribly faster similarly to how it was when I ran.

I looked overwhelmed at Varun and Sajay on my either sides.

I hugged both of them and came back to my place, looking at the door and for waiting for her to open the door.

They stood few steps behind me. Sajay got instantly busy texting someone; I know who that someone actually was. He couldn't help to wait or hear the word wait as well.

#Where's my love

Last Without Anything

Varun crossed his hands up against his chest, looked at me with a dreadful smile, throwing his sweat on the floor. He always hated to run a lot. I made him run a lot, made him feel bad.

We heard some sounds from the inside. It had sign of real human existence. Sajay slid the phone into his pocket.

I looked either sides, with confusion, happiness, contrastingly and literally every single emotion came in front of me.

The first lock went out. The first lock sound was heard, that was followed by crack sounds of the key being turned in its place.

I took a deep breath and opened my mouth and exhaled. I pushed my right fingers between my hair towards the right. I breathed out in front of my palm and checked my breath; not bad at this time of the day.

Both the locks on the door was unlocked.

I smiled and adjusted my shirt, pulled it down from either sides and cleared my throat.

#Where's my love

Last Without Anything

The door opened wide and I saw a man messed up in grey uniform, with a broom in his hands, looking at me, Varun and Sajay exhausted.

He was neither Aarti's father nor looked like any of her family men who almost look similar to her father. He was some outsider.

Sajay and Varun looked strangely.

I turned back and looked at Sajay and said, "Maybe one of the packers and shifters." I whispered the same looking around at Varun.

They both nodded their head.

I asked, "Is Mr. Nair here?"

The man looked confused. He didn't understand the name of the person, who I asked for.

I repeated again even more louder than before, "Can you call Mr. NAIR."

He seemed to have lost all the interest in the conversation with me. He looked numb. He failed to understand me.

#Where's my love

Last Without Anything

He looked in and called out something in some slang language that he originated from.

"It's Bengali for Sir please come here." Varun said. His mother's quarter half part lives in West Bengal. They know the language as his mother spent some of her childhood life there.

So happy to have a humble West Bengal friend; half friend I mean.

Some man walked towards the door, wearing a standard Arabic costume, cleaned to perfect white not lending a pinch of dirt on it.. He looked kind of rich. He might be the owner of the building.

"Hello Sir." Varun said in Bengali.

The Arabic sleek man didn't seem to understand his slang but the man in the grey uniform became excited on hearing his own language.The Arabic man looked confused.

I switched to the standard, "Assalamu Walaikum." in his language, I guessed is Arabic.

"Walaikum Assalam." He smiled.

#Where's my love

"*Do you know Mr. Nair?*" *I asked him.* "*Is he here? Can you please call him?*"

"*Ahh!*" *He exclaimed on hearing her father's name,* "*Nair... Yeah... I do know him... He left an hour back with his family.*"

I stood there shocked. The hair on my arms grew tall standing with emotion and pain. My eyes filled with tears, about to break down.

The Arabic man saw my eyes covered in redness of tears. He must have felt bad for me. He must have understood why I came here.

Sajay asked the Arabic man coming few steps forward, "*Do you know where they shifted to? Like where? Do you have the location map of Mr. Nair's new house?*"

The Arab man signed taking a deep breath out of his mouth, "*Well, I am afraid I cannot give you that information... Mr. Nair on the request of his first daughter told me not to reveal the location of their new house when some boys come and ask... I'm sorry... You can leave*

#Where's my love

now… I have a lot of work… I hope you understand."

The Arab man closed the door and locked it in reverse, two locks sounds waved into my ears. He understood everything.

I turned my head to the bell and looked an inch above the system. The name board of the tenant was removed. The board must have been taken but the screw holes, on the white plastered wall still remains.

That was how I felt.

I had to tell her that I like her. She kind of, partially knew that I like her, because of my dumb hinting reactions whenever she smiles or talks to me.

But the need to make it clear, urged me.

I rested my hand on the screw holes that was empty. I felt the coldness on the place. They left an hour back. One could not put a screw back into it with the hundred percentage assurance that it wouldn't fall.

#Where's my love

Last Without Anything

A mark made is not the same as it was before the mark. Her past made a mark on me. Her future brought a concern on me. I shivered in her thoughts as she passed away like a gentle breeze that I couldn't be with.

I wish I could see her again.

I want to slap her, ask her why she left. I want to hug her tight, chest to chest, heart to heart, for a lifetime. I want her beside me. I wanted her to be the first person who I talked to in the morning and the last person, at night.

Her insta account got deleted. Her phone number got deactivated. Her WhatsApp is not available. Her social links went down. She left just like that.

She left my life without keeping anything remaining, except the love I had for her.

#Where's my love

Hope you loved reading this short story.

Await for more amazing stories

-Arya Ramachandran

#Where's my love

Made in the USA
Middletown, DE
22 June 2023